HUMILIS

**Marie-Pascale Hardy** is a visual artist, poet and musician. Born 1985 in Quebec, Canada, she lived in London for nearly a decade where she released eight albums as singer of electronic duo Paco Sala. In 2015 she moved to Berlin to dedicate herself to her writing, art and spiritual practice. Now lives in France. *humilis* is her debut collection.

'Following the most sinuous path', *humilis* deviates in supple shapes through mind and matter, realising spare, subtle and often serene acts of metamorphosis.

— Sam Buchan-Watts, *Path Through Wood*

What you now have in front of you is a piece of light carved out of stone. Marie-Pascale Hardy's writing is tender and delicate, and yet, or precisely because of that, it is able to gracefully cross the boundary into the cruel. Like fingers slightly grazing a wound. After abandoning this book (because one can never finish reading a book, but only momentarily desert it), the reader is left not only with a sense of having gained a new language, but also, an experience. Like that of hanging in a hammock; suspended from the ground and yet, irremediably haunted by it. What you now have in front of you is the image of a woman caught in sight just before kneeling down to pray, of a pen caught in sight just before falling to the page. Only such writing can be called "humble", that is, magnificently truthful.

— Ramona de Jesús, *Dos metros cuadrados de piel*

Marie-Pascale Hardy's *humilis* is an exciting and unsettling read. The poems are at once earnest and wryly self-aware; they offer dispatches from life lived without the armour of cynicism; they detail the ecstasy and suffering of the moment, as well the sly humour of hindsight. The poems dismantle many of the usual hierarchies of desire, while they acknowledge how utterly we fall in love with other people – and lick our wounds privately – they also record an intense passion for the non-human, and offer lyric descriptions of being-in-the-world on the world's terms as much as one's own. The poems make linguistic fire from friction between the elemental and sardonic, between mystical integrity and the amused reality of everyday.

— Edward Doegar, *For Now*

In Marie-Pascale Hardy's *humilis,* a kind of brazen vulnerability, technical bravura and a sheer depth of humanity – itself all the more moving for its matter-of-fact presentation – are woven together into an astonishing, visceral, and incredibly beautiful, debut collection.

— Ahren Warner, *The sea is spread and cleaved and furled*

A wind from the sunrise… preceding a storm? Shaping predilections of the hanging tree: leaves and thick tapering branches bend back to reveal a bandaged body. Lines from the chest, placed in the ground, will themselves to be scavenged; lasting impressions are shiny, birdlike. Loath to leave unsubtle markers on the plain, Marie-Pascale Hardy's slender word-worms respect the dead silence with mutable signs.

— Sam Wilson Fletcher, *New Adjacent Possible Empty Niche*

There is a luminous, raw, almost physical quality to Hardy's poetry. It is melancholic and bitter, but pulls you in swirling unexpectedly with hope.

— Sahar Delijani, *Children Of The Jacaranda Tree*

# humilis

*Marie-Pascale Hardy*

Broken Sleep Books

ISBN: 978-1-915760-41-8

The author has asserted their right to be identified as the author of this Work in accordance with the Copyright, Designs and Patents Act 1988

Cover designed by Aaron Kent

Edited and Typeset by Aaron Kent

Broken Sleep Books Ltd
Rhydwen
Talgarreg
Ceredigion
SA44 4HB

Broken Sleep Books Ltd
Fair View
St Georges Road
Cornwall
PL26 7YH

# Contents

*To myself, in two hundred years*

# I

*We need nothing of what we have left behind*
— Amma Syncletica

*What I am saying sisters*
*is that the time is short*

*from now on those who have husbands*
*should live as if they had none*

*for this world in its present form*
*is passing away*

Waiting by the radiator for the last
load of sand to be poured
inside the flat

it's all been arranged

they've cut the running water
and the bathtub's filled to the brim
to enact a miraculous pond

in this arid home
populated only with scarce
thoughts of renunciation

the heater emits a comforting purr
and a warmth conducive to
contemplation

we still sleep in the same bunk
our backs to each other to
face god

In order to grow further
roots on this barren earth
we managed not to touch
became homeless with

a semblant of dignity
there is something about
you that cannot be held in
one palm without much
contortion

walls of ether roof of rains
*toi qui accepte tout ce que je*
& we trace a mild fence
between where we sit

face-to-face   cross-eyed
with a drop of water

Forced into nurturing
we are tired of meaning

articulate   lame
heavy

no longer welcomed we

cultivate a flavour that
grows from within

for the sake of our own
starvation

us   children of posterity!
well-fed   trained to breed

remain here   moan
and think we hold truth

tight   though its flow ceases
when hands are withdrawn

gestures of sympathy
are rendered obscene

from stiffness of joints

Only child

born on the cliff edge

once compared to mint   twice compared to rust
thrice compared to those who thrive on neglect

left content in the shade of pines
in a vain attempt to capture

circles of light dancing on
coats of needles

I became my own
sister-by-mistake

There *is* bliss in the sad
revelation in sanskrit

sleeping naked head into the east

we've come a long way
to sip its glory

        Salt
    in our eyes
sand between
our teeth
appearance of
density
    walking through
walls    flying under
the sea
    living outside the cycle
of dominance yet inside
that of dependency
        digging
    deeper
only to find a hole

## Outsight : View on a Wall

lost in musing over intricate

*vue à vol d'oiseau   tête en bas*

networks of dry
riverbeds   cracks
knots & fiberglass

*pendue   perpendiculaire au mur*

until ourself
begins to be
a bird

I dive in a bath so hot          skin turns
red in a second          I bear the burn
sink in and let          gravity
dissolve

my mind is in my chest          too
steamy          to think

I lie          unconscious
hair          comes alive

until somebody          tries to
open the door

no time          for shriveling

skillfully I          lift the plug
with toes          and remain
in the horizontal          position

*I am to enjoy*          *this until*
*the last*          *drop*

heavier          &          heavier

I stare at the white          mass of flesh
and feel the cold          air
reviving my          nipples

the water          like snow
uncovering          spring
corpses          and daffodils

Every morning I rehearse the death of my
mother   the death of my son   the death
of myself

in the dimness on my knees I whisper to
them what remained unsaid as if
they could hear me

lilies ablooming from all the tears &
ashes   my loved ones wilted
to soon be reduced to dust

whoever makes the wind turn
by some miracle always brings
them back before dusk

every evening I rehearse
their resurrection

I made space for you

emptiness

left the things that stood between us
behind    the colours    the faces    the vague
promises of safety    and it felt
nowhere near a sacrifice

we look alike in the dark

what we share on the surface    hardly
the odd peaks of a shimering truth
buried under loud voices

oblivion o precarious ecstasy
will you give me your hand for I
have no more nails to ravage

avid grazer of ethereal
foliage    jaws & articulations
aching since to love is to kneel
is to surrender to surreal
unpredictable forces

I made space for you

emptiness

you didn't wait to be asked twice
to grow and swallow me whole
so I ghosted you

You were to follow the mountain
or else the mountain would
follow you

you were to stand by the cliff
and lean towards
the ocean

let yourself fall backwards
trust the wind
to hold you

Now reading only

scriptures in braille
with the tip

of tongue

She often has these dialogues with her selves
full of having-said-thats and contradictions

      cornflakes
    confetti

*insanity-which-is-also-death*

transcribing her visions into common English
she rejoices: nowhere is she expected

*bedridden, entranced*

rises only to advise troubled visitors
from the outside world

she's got too much time on her hands
too little weight on her shoulders

of her spring-branch fingers
she painstakingly bites the buds

*bleeding-which-is-also-death*

sometimes I like that she talks so much
it means I can look at her more

I can look at her *leafless arms*

at that time of the day when the window
turns into a mirror

## Eye Exercise I

make sure you look outside now & then to make sure
you live inside at least now & then make sure the lake is
still where it was last time you looked outside to make
sure you lived inside & the lake was where it is now

## Of Leaves

you are like those stand
ing straight in the middle
of a field with no one to
lean on    like those standing
still   against the wind thick
ens their skin and as they un
fold form a shield of leaves
like those standing strong
for winters here are long
who else to keep them
warm but their
own wood

# Willy-Willly

in the metaphoric country of your mind
cities emerge to die at once in a hurricane
of thoughts    a mountain on every heartbeat
slips into the ocean    another island forms
and after countless wars finally declares
independence
an era of serenity follows    nature takes
back its motherly role    the people adorn a
newborn innocence and so as to purge themselves
of bitter reminiscence    reenact this ancient
tradition
every autumn    women and men    young and
aged    gather on the hill at dawn    invariably
dressed in black    weep and wail the sorrows
of the past as trees shed their vivid burden
and wild boar & deer bow down in
reverence    until grievance is lifted
*rainbowssmilesshootingstarsparakeetsfireworks*
long forgotten are the storms    the servitude
the drought    peace has spun a soft cocoon
around the skies    a maiden milks a goat while
fisherwomen sail seawards    regardless of race
or creed    everybody whistles the same tune
in unison
only few houses are shaken when a bout
of hiccups wreaks havoc    an imperceptible
fissure forms on the rocky shore    before all
goes to stillness    a thick silence stretches
like winter fog at dusk    even the wind
retires to its chambers

but as you lay in bed waiting for sleep
in the distance   a subtle hum arises    not one
you hear    but feel within your entire
body    doubt creeps in   dividing the people
into separate camps according to whom they
choose to blame
despite the warnings of the elderly about
the dangers of fragmentation and the measures
taken to numb agitation   the fissure enlarges
noticeably    soon the island splits into small
pieces floating adrift on troubled waters
on one of which you are sitting
unimpressed   you have seen it all before
may this time be the last    your body dissolves
from extremity to core until all around and
inside turns pitch black
yet untenably luminous
you squint to discern the horizon    there is
none    you squint to discern the tip of
your nose    there is none    you squint
until there is no more eye to squint
with    until there is no more
I to witness the void
until there is no

# II

*of the person who can be seen*
*to stumble & who falls with joy, unhurt*
— J.H. Prynne

# Vertigo

for once
make real the curse
you prophesy
not-knowing
distance nor
consequences

fearing less
what's below
than the heights
unconquered

gravity   unfurl!

saturated with vain
*mondanités*   utterly
insolvent   reliant on
a lover's alms

embracing downwardness

o this little twitch I give
just before hitting the
ground

visceral contusion

will *not*
for once
wake upon
arrival

on you thick pile of dead
leaves   promise of
salvation

## Faiblesse

hold onto who comes first
strips of velvet snaking their
way in through muscles & veins
envious of tonsils   kidneys   ovaries
surely the heart craves a companion
two lungs lush with thorns & rotten twigs
   the injured require a bond
hold onto who comes first
in other words   *deviate*

# Flying

or rather floating

landing   breaking   dying
rotting   sprouting   growing

climbing all around a trunk already ripe
feeding on its sap

spiraling   forever rising
following the most sinuous path

leading to the sky

We

*Literally, 'bent to the ground',
i.e. inclined to the lowest place.*
*– St. Thomas Aquinas*

Let the ocean grow and
swallow the world—

Plant a mirror
on the beach.




(fooling seagulls)

## Nocturne (D)


a field with trees around.


I decide to run down the hill, following
the road. Only just escaping the fall from
grace into love; this ditch being a common
mistake. Out of politeness end up accepting
a lift from a young child learning to drive.
Half an hour to get out of the car park.
I need to be away from home for a while,
severely adrift for no good reason.
Parasiting, house versus catsitting,
abusing friends, testing their hospitality by
stretching the length of my stay without
notice. My belongings fit in one rucksack—
I believe it must be waterproof. My
creations I dispose of as they hatch
then sit in the corner and drool.
I deviate.
                    Like a tree growing wonky around a fence.
I'm writing this essay on altruism and the
aim is not wrapped in foil and glitter nor
to prove a point. It is the reconciliation
with the nature of oneness or *interlinkage*.
I don't listen to much music while I write.
I worry about porosity a lot. I stay away
from the source of inspiration. The drop
of ink that pollutes the water. The unfolding
of the hidden order. Muses are poison.
I keep them away from my tongue.

I find myself in a large room where plenty
of furnitures—which I did not choose—
are assembled. The floor is dirty. The wall
is dirty. The chair is dirty. The water is dirty.
The mouth is dry. Desire is building up.
I go to the bathroom for quick relief
but the door is made of glass and does not
lock. I am wholly naked when a dozen
strangers come to visit. *Despite appearances,
we are beings without borders*. My skin is made
of glass and does not lock. I am wholly
naked when a dozen strangers come to visit.
Indiscriminately I turn them all on, strangers
and fridges and washing machines...

A pile of appliances in the middle of

Out fishing for friends
as soon as the season opens
quite a bravery to come back
after such failure    it's the period
of shedding skins   of offing layers of
old    see who's eager to die in your hands
who has nothing but groundless hope
marvel at the sight of their blood
at the absence of fear    or is this
lake in fact a pool of tears
then enjoy peace after
decapitulation

m        e        a        n        d        e        r

Just like a snake I crave the burn the summer traces on my skin on every glimpse the sun may seize of it as it peels away and the new delays its thickening—despite a certain swelling thirst and a sane amount of wariness. As we walk on the sunny side at snail pace and trail our sugarcoated legs and slime, my ankles turn relentlessly. *Would we hold hands, would we, if we were sure to get it back afterwards?* No. Now: isn't this bus stop a safe place, a haven for poultry's remains where I shall pompously declare: *Communism looks good on you* (even though your faith has faded). Spit—thrown off bridges and balustrades, travels by means of gravity, through time, and sometimes hangs in mid-air, defying expectancy. When you say *I love you*, I say *of course, who wouldn't*, betraying disbelief. Shade—in woodlands, shed its flattering light shyly on one side of your face, hiding rings and wrinkles. The B-side of mine grinds against the rocks and the eyes go milky; erosion scatters our scales around. Stray dogs follow us to the cliff edge in a crocodile line until we run out of food

## Englués

    chicken bones   cigarettes
dead leaves

    *elles vous enjambent   ivres
et ingrates*

    the daughters of middle-
aged slugs

## Eye Exercise II

gaze intently at what is right in front of you    lifting
the grey veil of thoughts with the index finger and
thumb of the right hand    revel in kind scrutiny
they are many looking through your eyes

This diluted sunset
laid out before us once we reached
our first unobstructed view over the hills
when snow was a thing of the past
and you complained about the trees
along the way obscuring the sight
despite its most demure intentions
was gripping

You know me like a sister knows
her way through the woods
despite overgrowth    you know me
like a sister knows
where to grope

I was hoping for a spectacular sunrise
    awakening by your side as I drew the
      curtains of the window with breath
        taking view over roofs and the city
        opulent and flat like a sea that
      meets in clandestinity her
    lover the sky
but all I saw was disappointment
forgetting it's winter
and your window
faces north

Sitting on a large bed or was it the floor
there was your girlfriend your friends and a
    boy I hadn't seen since primary school
they were commenting on something like
    a football match or a terrorist attack
you were discussing facts since you are
    way above opinions and emotivity

drowsy

my forehead gradually made its
    way to your shoulder

        the sound of my heart
    the path of my breath
in all its intricacies

I synced mine to yours and in between
    each breath we met in pure

        fuzzy
cocoon

You dive into my bed. My bed
is a sea. A sea that swirls and
swallows. Swallows limbs
into sleep.

Your leap, head first, increases
ripples, waving wrinkles
in the sheets.

Lesson learned one stormy night:
*To hold my pillow tight.*

At sea pervades a loneliness.
For those who do not
dare to drown
foerever float adrift.

You dive into my bed. My bed
is a sea. I am one with the
mattress. You dive
into me.

Prayer from the Island of Feathers:
*May the full moon pull you close*
*or by low tide your body*
*be found*

Opium had made you more feline.

In the haze of a rising sun countless particles of dust
rehearsed a chaotic sequence in slow motion while you
went on rubbing yourself against the walls of my skin,
crawling on the floor of my skin, claws withdrawn,
undignified, heavy. Purring for a feed, a stroke.

Dawn plead innocence; the fumes had delayed its
punctual awakings.

Unattended, with your sex—nascent—I contented
myself, famished. Rode it and handled it as if it
were my own.

In near darkness softly infused in a stream of shallow
dreams of decline.

I woke up convinced of my own irresistibility.

Already you were spread bare rambling all over me.
Your lips were those of all the girls I'd ever kissed
— *soft slippery surfaces precise loose coated with glue* —
and your eyes shone the same distinct humid intent
of not letting go.

of not letting go...
with disgust I had to use my nails to scrape you off
and let you out in the rain

The sky was low and understanding—
heavy blanket thrown upon the cityscape.

Having left the house in the need for
alleviation, I looked up incredulous

and recognised his appeal: a greyness
mistaken for a sign of maturity.

Along with a smooth breeze he came
real close to my face and whispered

*Turn around.*

And so I knew he would do me a favour
at the back of the car, without protection.

I let him, out of curiosity.

For celestial intercourse involves no
betrayal and leads to abundant crop

I am a child, entering a room.

Adults of various dimensions
seated around a large oval
table. All strangers except
one. They stop talking, look
down on me. My mother
stands up, comes closer.
I am very small. Dirt under
the nails. She leans towards
me with a sinister, mocking
smile. She is very tall. Index
finger erect she pokes my
stomach with a loud, cruel
laugh. Everybody joins in,
exchanges conniving glances.
Each stab makes me shrink to
a ridiculous size and the pain
feels unbearably real

I dream of the night all my lovers unite.

Nude in a circle dance around me naked,
glued at the hips so the roots are shaken;
like everyone's rowing at the same pace
and gay.

The dance may be frantic, may be loose.

I, alone in the eye of the storm, budlike,
pacified. Resting among the hurts.
While all around me they spin
and spin so fast all I can
see is a single horse galloping in
slow motion; his hooves at times
suspended in the air.

Mesmerized I fail to notice
we're all entangled in a web
of invisible things; no one knows
who's the spider who's the prey.
Just a pile of lean fuzzy legs
interlaced, complicated.

I am enjoying the confusion
when all at once they
attack me with care
precise, dactylous
until I culminate.

*The same spasmodic opening is observed in the rose*

## Accolade

I go to the bathroom for quick relief
but the door is made of glass and does not
lock. I am wholly naked when a two year-old
already acting like a biped enters the flat using
his own set of keys. We embrace. I inquire about
his day. He went to the swimming pool, he says.
I confess my envy. What incredible independence,
eloquence, at such a young age. I can talk about
anything with my boy!
Now sitting on the rocking chair by the window
giving onto grey empty streets depicted with
straight lines and smooth surfaces, all stainless
steel-like. I am holding him near my heart.
We are both naked but his skin
is warmer than mine

Victor,

This epitomizes you.
Immense statue. Broken
nose. Missing head.
*This body a condensation of all concrete possibilities.*
Waking up from trying
to shout. Bizarrely
punitive

# NOTES

p.9 Desert Mother St. Syncletica the Righteous of Alexandria, *Apophthegmata Patrum* (c.480–500)

p.11 First [Trans-]Corinthians 7:29

p.13 transl. 'you who accept everything that I'

p.18 transl. 'bird's eye view, head down / hung, perpendicular to the wall'

p.24 in italics, except '*leafless arms*' – Caroline Walker Bynum, *Holy Feast and Holy Fast, The Religious Significance of Food to Medieval Women*, University of California Press (1988)

'leafless arms' – Jones Very, "The Tree", *Essays And Poems*, (Boston: Charles C. Little And James Brown, MDCCCXXXIX), p. 119.

p.29 J.H. Prynne, "Quality in that Case as Pressure", *The White Stones* (1969), Poems, Bloodaxe (2015), p. 78

p.35 St. Thomas Aquinas, *Summa Theologica*, Pt. II-II, Q. 161, Art. I (1485) – "a humble man is so called because he is, as it were, 'humo acclinis'" [*Literally, 'bent to the ground'], i.e. inclined to the lowest place. This may happen in two ways. First, through an extrinsic principle, for instance when one is cast down by another, and thus humility is a punishment. Secondly, through intrinsic principle: and this may be done sometimes well, for instance when a man, considering his own failings, assumes the lowest place according to his mode: thus Abraham said to the Lord (Gn. 18:27), "I will speak to my Lord, whereas I am dust and ashes." In this way humility is a virtue. Sometimes, however, this may be ill-done, for instance when man, "not understanding his honor, compares himself to senseless beasts, and becomes like to them" (Ps. 48:13)"

p.39     '*Despite appearances, we are beings without borders*' – Michael Talbot, *The Holographic Universe*, HarperCollins Publishers (1996)

p.42     transl. 'slimed / they crawl over you, drunk / and ungrateful'

p.52     '*The same spasmodic opening is observed in the rose*' – A.G.L. Hellyer, Simple Rose Growing, W. H. & L. Collingridge Ltd (1957)

# ACKNOWLEDGEMENTS

Much gratitude to the editors of following publications where some of these poems were first published : *Poetry London, SAND Journal, FU Review, stadtsprachen, Anthropocene, Life Lines - EggBox Publishing, PERVERSE.*

Much gratitude to the following artist residencies where some of these poems came to life : Arteles, Villa Sarkia, Zaratan – Arte Contemporânea.

Much gratitude to all beings, big or small, near or far, human or non-human, friends or ennemies, visible or invisible. Sorry if I forget anyone.

# LAY OUT YOUR UNREST

www.ingramcontent.com/pod-product-compliance
Lightning Source LLC
Chambersburg PA
CBHW030155070426
42447CB00032B/1205